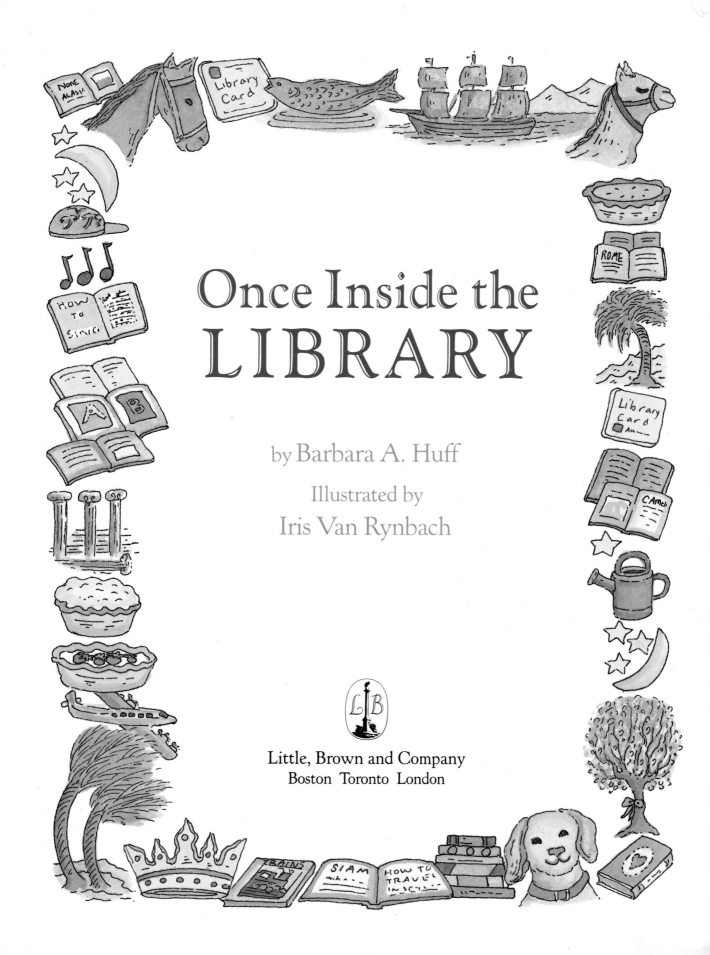

Once Inside the
LIBRARY

by Barbara A. Huff

Illustrated by

Iris Van Rynbach

Little, Brown and Company
Boston Toronto London

First edition

Library of Congress Cataloging-in-Publication Data

Huff, Barbara A.
    Once inside the library / by Barbara A. Huff: illustrated by
Iris Van Rynbach. — 1st ed.

    p. cm.
    Summary: A verse evocation of the joys of books, libraries, and
reading.
    ISBN 0-316-37967-0
    1. Libraries — Juvenile poetry. 2. Books and reading — Juvenile
poetry. 3. Children's poetry, American. [1. Libraries — Poetry.
2. Books and reading — Poetry. 3. American poetry.] I. Van
Rynbach, Iris, ill. II. Title.
PS3558.U318L54   1990
811'.54 — dc20   89–12131
                                                        CIP
                                                        AC

10 9 8 7 6 5 4 3 2

NIL

*Published simultaneously in Canada
by Little, Brown & Company (Canada) Limited*

Paintings done in watercolor and pen and ink on Arches watercolor paper
Color separations made by New Interlitho, Milan, Italy
Text set in Kennerly by Litho Composition Company, Inc.
Printed and bound by New Interlitho, Milan, Italy

For John David Ridge,
first-class all the way

And for Katie Diakiw,
who discovered "The Library" when she was nine

B. H.

For James F. McAndrews,
who loves books

I. V. R.

It looks like any building
when you pass it on the street,
made of stone and glass and marble,
made of iron and concrete.

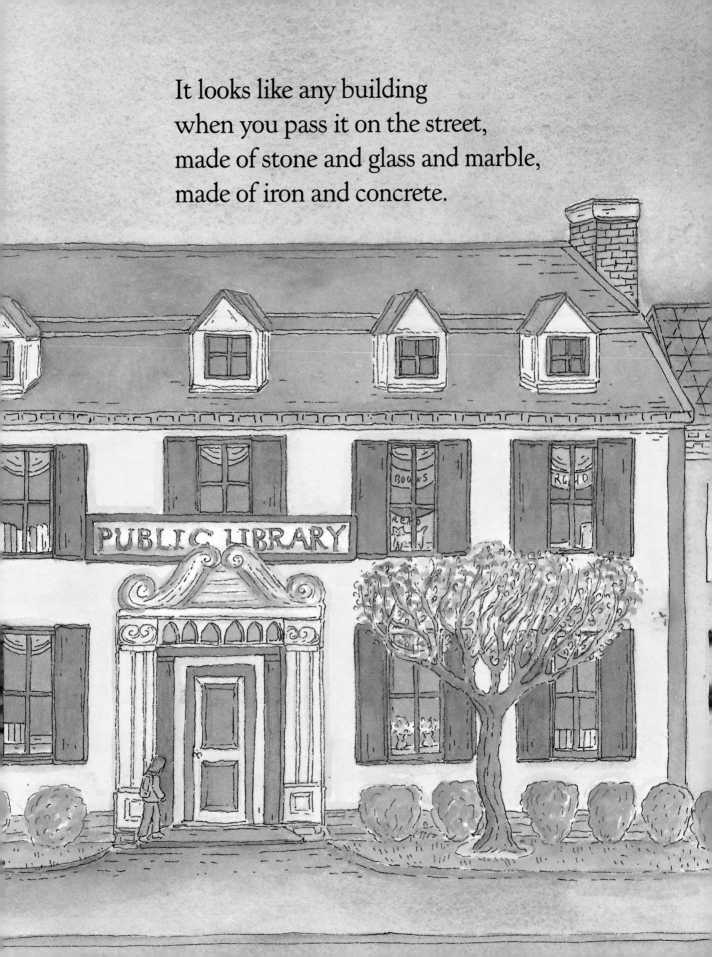

But once inside . . .

You can ride a camel

or a train,

visit Rome,

Siam,

or Nome,

feel a hurricane,

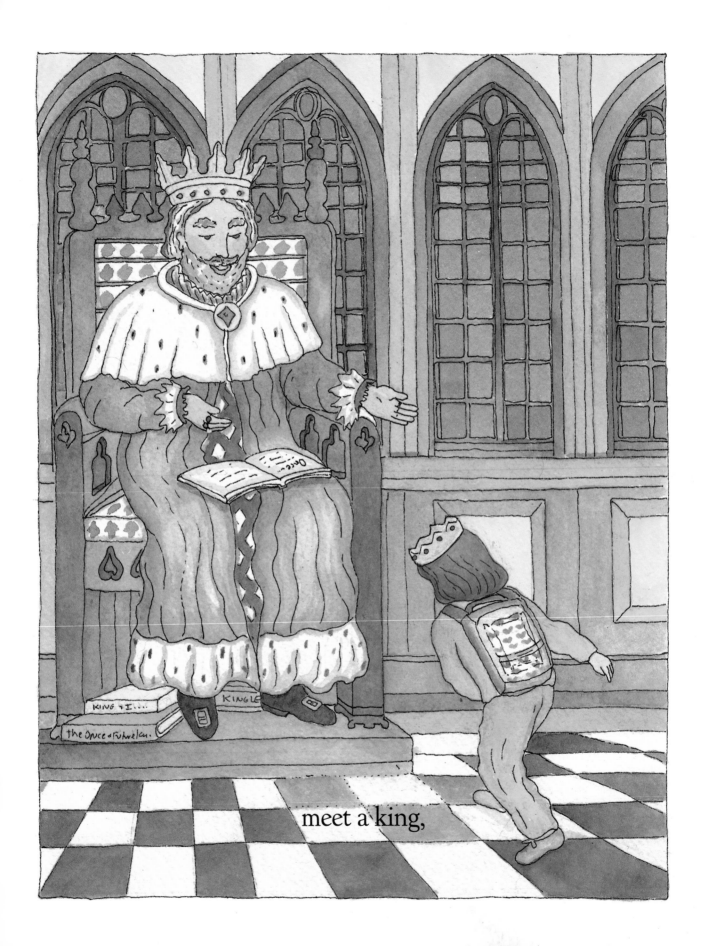

meet a king,

learn to sing,

how to bake a pie,

go to sea,

plant a tree,

find how airplanes fly,

train a horse, and of course
have all the dogs you'd like,

see the moon,

a sandy dune,

or catch a whopping pike.

Everything that books can bring
you'll find inside those walls.
A world is there for you to share
when adventure calls.

You cannot tell its magic
by the way the building looks,

but there's wonderment within it —
the wonderment of books.